Conference of the North American Chapter of the Association for Computational Linguistics: Human Language Technologies 2016 (NAACL HLT 2016)

Tutorial Abstracts

San Diego, California, USA
12 – 17 June 2016

ISBN: 978-1-5108-2515-4

Printed from e-media with permission by:

Curran Associates, Inc.
57 Morehouse Lane
Red Hook, NY 12571

Some format issues inherent in the e-media version may also appear in this print version.

Printed by Curran Associates, Inc. (2016)

Association for Computational Linguistics
209 N. Eighth Street
Stroudsburg, Pennsylvania 18360

Phone: 1-570-476-8006
Fax: 1-570-476-0860

acl@aclweb.org

Additional copies of this publication are available from:

Curran Associates, Inc.
57 Morehouse Lane
Red Hook, NY 12571 USA
Phone: 845-758-0400
Fax: 845-758-2634
Email: curran@proceedings.com
Web: www.proceedings.com

NAACL HLT 2016

The 2016 Conference of the North American Chapter of the Association for Computational Linguistics: Human Language Technologies

Tutorial Abstracts

June 12-17, 2016
San Diego, California, USA

Introduction

This volume contains the abstracts for the tutorials presented at NAACL 2016. Tutorials were selected by joint call for NAACL, ACL and EMNLP. Together we accepted 6 NAACL tutorials out of a total of 32 joint submissions.

We would like to thank Kevin Knight (NAACL general chair), Jason Riesa (NAACL website chair), Adam Lopez and Margaret Mitchell (NAACL publications chairs), and Priscilla Rasmussen (local arrangement chair) for their help during the whole process. We also want to extend our sincere gratitude to the other tutorial chairs who helped with reviewing: Rebecca Hwa, Bishan Yang, Alexandra Birch, and Willem Zuidema.

Enjoy the tutorials!
NAACL 2016 Tutorial Co-chairs
Alexander M Rush
Mohit Bansal

Tutorial Co-chairs:

Alexander M. Rush, Harvard University
Mohit Bansal, TTI-Chicago

Table of Contents

Conference Program

Sunday, June 12, 2016

Morning Session

9:00–12:30 *English Resource Semantics*
Dan Flickinger, Emily M. Bender and Woodley Packard

9:00–12:30 *Multilingual Multimodal Language Processing Using Neural Networks*
Mitesh M. Khapra and Sarath Chandar

9:00–12:30 *Question Answering with Knowledge Base, Web and Beyond*
Wen-tau Yih and Hao Ma

12:30–2:00 ***Break***

Afternoon Session

2:00–5:30 *Recent Progress in Deep Learning for NLP*
Zhengdong Lu and Hang Li

2:00–5:30 *Scalable Statistical Relational Learning for NLP*
William Yang Wang and William Cohen

2:00–5:30 *Statistical Machine Translation between Related Languages*
Pushpak Bhattacharyya, Mitesh M. Khapra and Anoop Kunchukuttan

English Resource Semantics

Instructors: Dan Flickinger, Emily M. Bender, and Woodley Packard

Abstract:

Recent years have seen a dramatic increase in interest in semantically-informed natural language processing, including parsing into semantic representations, grounded language processing that connects linguistic structures to world representations, proposals to integrate compositional and distributional approaches to semantics, and approaches to semantically-sensitive tasks including sentiment analysis, summarization, generation, machine translation, and information extraction which take into account linguistic structure beyond n-grams. The semantic inputs to this work include a wide range of representations, from word embeddings, to syntactic dependencies used as a proxy for semantic dependencies, to sentence-level semantic representations either partial (e.g. semantic role labels) or fully articulated.

The purpose of this tutorial is to make accessible an important resource in this space, namely the semantic representations produced by the English Resource Grammar (ERG; Flickinger 2000, 2011). The ERG is a broad-coverage, linguistically motivated precision grammar for English, associating richly detailed semantic representations with input sentences. These representations, dubbed English Resource Semantics or ERS, are in the formalism of Minimal Recursion Semantics (MRS; Copestake et al 2005). They include not only semantic roles, but also information about the scope of quantifiers and scopal operators including negation, as well as semantic representations of linguistically complex phenomena such as time and date expressions, conditionals, and comparatives (Flickinger et al, 2014). ERS can be expressed in various ways, including a logic-based syntax using predicates and arguments, dependency graphs and dependency triples. In addition, the representations can be obtained either from existing manually produced annotations over texts from a variety of genres (the Redwoods Treebank, Oepen et al 2004) and DeepBank (Wall Street Journal corpus: Flickinger et al 2012) or by processing new text with the ERG and its associated parsing and parse selection algorithms.

With high parsing accuracy with rich semantic representations, English Resource Semantics is a valuable source of information for many semantically-sensitive NLP tasks. ERS-based systems have achieved state-of-the-art results in various tasks, including the identification of speculative or negated event mentions in biomedical text (MacKinlay et al 2011), question generation (Yao et al 2012), detecting the scope of negation (Packard et al 2014), relating natural language to robot control language (Packard 2014), and recognizing textual entailment (PETE task; Lien & Kouylekov 2015). ERS representations have also been beneficial in semantic transfer-based MT (Oepen et al 2007, Bond et al 2011), ontology acquisition (Herbelot 2006), extraction of glossary sentences

(Reiplinger et al 2012), sentiment analysis (Kramer & Gordon 2014), and the ACL Anthology Searchbench (Schäfer et al 2011).

The goal of this tutorial is to make this resource more accessible to the ACL community. Specifically, we take as our learning goals that tutorial participants will learn how to: (1) set up the ERG-based parsing stack, including preprocessing; (2) access ERG Redwoods/DeepBank treebanks in the various export formats; and (3) interpret ERS representations.

Outline

- Overview of goals and methods [10 min]
- Implementation platform and formalism [30 min]
    - Installation of parser and grammar on participants' laptops
    - Parsing sample data to produce ERS (English Resource Semantics) output
    - Introduction to ERS formalism
- Treebanks and output formats [30 min]
    - Search tools over manually annotated corpora
    - Available output formats and conversion utilities
    - Disambiguation alternatives: one-best or manual
- Semantic phenomena [20 min]
    - Exploration of linguistic analyses for selected phenomena
    - Documentation of semantic representations
- Coffee break
- Semantic phenomena (continued) [20 min]
- Parameter tuning for applications [20 min]
    - Parser settings for genre, domain, precision, resource limits
    - Robust processing for out-of-grammar inputs
    - Efficiency vs. precision
- Future enhancements underway [30 min]
    - Word senses for finer-grained semantic representations
    - More derivational morphology (e.g.\ semi-productive deverbal nouns)
    - Support for coreference within and across sentence boundaries
- Sample applications using ERS [20 min]

About the Instructors

Dan Flickinger, Stanford University, danf@stanford.edu, http://lingo.stanford.edu/danf

Dan Flickinger is a Senior Research Associate at CSLI at Stanford, and manager of the Linguistic Grammars Online (LinGO) Laboratory, where he is the principal developer of the LinGO English Resource Grammar (ERG), a precise broad-coverage implementation of HPSG. His primary research interests are in wide-coverage grammar engineering for both parsing and generation, lexical representation, the syntax-semantics interface, methodology for evaluation of semantically precise grammars, and practical applications of 'deep' processing. Applied and industrial experience includes co-founding the software company YY Technologies, which from 2000-2002 sold automated consumer email response technology incorporating the ERG; and since 2009 developing online educational software using the ERG for teaching English writing skills, first as part of the Education Program for Gifted Youth (EPGY) at Stanford, and for the past three years as a senior researcher at the EPGY spin-off company Redbird Advanced Learning, based in Oakland, California.

Emily M. Bender, University of Washington, ebender@uw.edu,
http://faculty.washington.edu/ebender

Emily M. Bender is a Professor in the Department of Linguistics and Associate Professor in the Department of Computer Science & Engineering at the University of Washington. Her primary research interests lie in multilingual grammar engineering, semantic representations, and the incorporation of linguistic knowledge, especially from semantics and linguistic typology, in computational linguistics. She is the primary developer of the Grammar Matrix grammar customization system, which is developed in the context of the DELPH-IN Consortium (Deep Linguistic Processing with HPSG Initiative). Her book, *Linguistic Fundamentals for Natural Language Processing: 100 Essentials from Morphology and Syntax* grew out of a NAACL 2012 tutorial on that topic.

Woodley Packard, University of Washington, sweaglesw@sweaglesw.org,
http://sweaglesw.org/linguistics/about/

Woodley Packard is a student at the University of Washington, pursuing a PhD in Computational Linguistics with Emily M. Bender. His research interests include efficient algorithms for grammar-based parsing, generation, annotation, and learning; robustness mechanisms for precision grammars; methodologies for contextually-informed disambiguation; and applications of semantic representations. He wrote and maintains the ACE parser/generator and the FFTB annotation tool. Recent work includes designing and building the top-performing entry for SemEval 2014 Task 6 on interpreting natural language commands to robots.

References

Bond, F., Oepen, S., Nichols, E., Flickinger, D., Velldal, E., & Haugereid, P. (2011). Deep open-sourc emachine translation. Machine Translation , 25 , 87-105. doi: 10.1007/s10590-011-9099-4

Copestake, A., Flickinger, D., Pollard, C., & Sag, I. A. (2005). Minimal Recursion Semantics. An introduction. Research on Language and Computation, 3(4), 281-332.

Flickinger, D. (2000). On building a more efficient grammar by exploiting types. Natural Language Engineering, 6 (1), 15-28.

Flickinger, D. (2011). Accuracy vs. robustness in grammar engineering. In E. M. Bender & J. E. Arnold (Eds.), Language from a cognitive perspective: Grammar, usage, and processing (pp. 31-50). Stanford: CSLI Publications.

Flickinger, D., Bender, E. M., & Oepen, S. (2014). Towards an encyclopedia of compositional semantics: Documenting the interface of the english resource grammar. In N. Calzolari et al. (Eds.), Proceedings of the ninth international conference on language resources and evaluation (LREC'14) (pp. 875-881). Reykjavik, Iceland: European Language Resources Association (ELRA).

Flickinger, D., Zhang, Y., & Kordoni, V. (2012). DeepBank. A dynamically annotated treebank of the Wall Street Journal. In (p. 85-96). Lisbon, Portugal: Edições Colibri.

Herbelot, A., & Copestake, A. (2006). Acquiring Ontological Relationships from Wikipedia Using RMRS. In Proceedings of the ISWC 2006 workshop on web content.

Ivanova, A., Oepen, S., Dridan, R., Flickinger, D., & Øvrelid, L. (2013). On different approaches to syntactic analysis into bi-lexical dependencies. An empirical comparison of direct, PCFG-based, and HPSG-based parsers. In Proceedings of the 13th International Conference on Parsing Technologies (p. 63-72). Nara, Japan.

Kramer, J., & Gordon, C. (2014). Improvement of a naive bayes sentiment classifier using mrs-based features. In Proceedings of the third joint conference on lexical and computational semantics (*SEM 2014) (pp. 22-29). Dublin, Ireland: Association for Computational Linguistics and Dublin City University.

Lien, E., & Kouylekov, M. (2015). Semantic parsing for textual entailment. In Proceedings of the 14th International Conference on Parsing Technologies (p. 40-49). Bilbao, Spain.

MacKinlay, A., Martinez, D., & Baldwin, T. (2011). A parser-based approach to detecting modification of biomedical events. In Proceedings of the acm fifth international workshop on data and text mining in biomedical informatics (pp. 51-58). New York, NY, USA: ACM.

Miyao, Y., Oepen, S., & Zeman, D. (2014). In-House. An ensemble of pre-existing off-the-shelf parsers. In Proceedings of the 8th International Workshop on Semantic Evaluation (p. 63-72). Dublin, Ireland.

Oepen, S., Flickinger, D., Toutanova, K., & Manning, C. D. (2004). LinGO Redwoods. A rich and dynamic treebank for HPSG. Research on Language and Computation, 2(4), 575-596.

Oepen, S., Velldal, E., Lnning, J. T., Meurer, P., Rosn, V., & Flickinger, D. (2007). Towards hybrid quality-oriented machine translation: On linguistics and probabilities in MT. In Proceedings of 11th conference on theoretical and methodological issues in machine translation (p. 144-153). Skvde, Sweden.

Packard, W. (2014). UW-MRS: Leveraging a deep grammar for robotic spatial commands. In Proceedings of the 8th international workshop on semantic evaluation (semeval 2014) (pp. 812-816). Dublin, Ireland: Association for Computational Linguistics and Dublin City University.

Packard, W., Bender, E. M., Read, J., Oepen, S., & Dridan, R. (2014). Simple negation scope resolution through deep parsing: A semantic solution to a semantic problem. In Proceedings of the 52nd annual meeting of the association for computational linguistics (volume 1: Long papers) (pp. 69-78). Baltimore, Maryland: Association for Computational Linguistics.

Reiplinger, M., Schäfer, U., & Wolska, M. (2012). Extracting glossary sentences from scholarly articles: A comparative evaluation of pattern bootstrapping and deep analysis. In Proceedings of the ACL-2012 special workshop on rediscovering 50 years of discoveries (pp. 55-65). Jeju Island, Korea.

Schäfer, U., Kiefer, B., Spurk, C., Steffen, J., & Wang, R. (2011). The ACL Anthology Searchbench. In Proceedings of the ACL-HLT 2011 system demonstrations (pp. 7-13). Portland, Oregon: Association for Computational Linguistics.

Yao, X., Bouma, G., & Zhang, Y. (2012). Semantics-based question generation and implementation. Dialogue & Discourse, 3(2), 11-42.

Multilingual Multimodal Language Processing Using Neural Networks

Instructors: Mitesh M Khapra and Sarath Chandar

Abstract:

We live in an increasingly multilingual multimodal world where it is common to find multiple views of the same entity across modalities and languages. For example, news articles which get published in multiple languages are essentially different views of the same entity. Similarly, video, audio and multilingual subtitles are multiple views of the same movie clip. Given the proliferation of such multilingual multimodal content it is no longer sufficient to process a single modality or language at a time. Specifically, there is an increasing demand for allowing transfer, conversion and access across such multiple views of the data. For example, users want to translate/convert news articles to their native language, automatically caption their travel photos and even ask natural language questions over videos and images. This has led to a lot of excitement around this interdisciplinary research area which requires ideas from Machine Learning, Natural Language Processing, Speech and Computer Vision among other fields.

In this tutorial we focus on neural network based models for addressing various problems in this space. We will first introduce the participants to some of the basic concepts and building blocks that such approaches rely on. We will then describe some of these approaches in detail. There are two important parts to the tutorial. In the first part, we will talk about approaches which aim to learn a common representation for entities across languages and modalities thereby enabling cross lingual and cross modal access and transfer. In the second part we will talk about multilingual multimodal generation. For example, we will discuss neural network based approaches which aim at (i) generating translations in multiple languages, (ii) generating images given a natural language description and (iii) generating captions in multiple languages.

Outline:

1. Introduction and Motivation [20 mins]
2. Basics [40 mins]
    1. Learning distributed representations using Neural Networks
    2. Convolutional Neural Networks
    3. Recursive Neural Networks and its variants
3. Multilingual/Multimodal Representation Learning [40 mins]
    1. Using parallel data with and without word alignments
    2. Using pivot view in the absence of parallel data
4. Multilingual/Multimodal Generation [80 mins]
    1. Neural Machine Translation systems
    2. Generating captions from images
    3. Answering natural language questions over images

    4. Describing videos
    5. Generating images from a given natural language description
5. Summary

About the Instructors:

Mitesh M Khapra: IBM Research India, mikhapra@in.ibm.com,
http://researcher.watson.ibm.com/researcher/view.php?person=in-mikhapra

Mitesh Khapra obtained his Ph.D. from the Indian Institute of Technology, Bombay in the area of Natural Language Processing with a focus on reusing resources for multilingual computation. His areas of interest include Statistical Machine Translation, Text Analytics, Crowdsourcing, Argument Mining and Deep Learning. He is currently working as a Researcher at IBM Research India where he is focusing on mining arguments from large unstructured text. He is also interested in learning common representations across languages and modalities with the view of enabling cross language and cross modal access. He has co-authored papers in top NLP and ML conferences such as ACL, NAACL, EMNLP, AAAI and NIPS.

Sarath Chandar: University of Montreal, apsarathchandar@gmail.com, http://sarathchandar.in/

Sarath Chandar is currently a PhD student in University of Montreal where he works with Yoshua Bengio and Hugo Larochelle on Deep Learning for complex NLP tasks like question answering and dialog systems. His research interests includes Machine Learning, Natural Language Processing, Deep Learning, and Reinforcement Learning. Before joining University of Montreal, he was a Blue Scholar in IBM Research India for a year.

Question Answering with Knowledge Base, Web and Beyond

Scott Wen-tau Yih & Hao Ma
Microsoft Research

Introduction

Developing a Question Answering (QA) system to automatically answer natural-language questions has been a long-standing research problem since the dawn of AI, for its clear practical and scientific value. For instance, whether a system can answer questions correctly is a natural way to evaluate a machine's understanding of a domain. Providing succinct and precise answers to informational queries is also the direction pursued by the next generation of search engines that aim to incorporate more "semantics", as well as the basic function in digital assistants like Siri and Cortana.

In this tutorial, we aim to give the audience a coherent overview of the research of question answering. We will first introduce a variety of QA problems proposed by pioneer researchers and briefly describe the early efforts. By contrasting with the current research trend in this domain, the audience can easily comprehend what technical problems remain challenging and what the main breakthroughs and opportunities are during the past half century. For the rest of the tutorial, we select three categories of the QA problems that have recently attracted a great deal of attention in the research community, and will present the tasks with the latest technical survey.

The first two categories regard answering factoid questions, where the main difference of the problem settings is the information source used for extracting answers. *QA with knowledge base* aims to answer natural language questions using real-world facts stored in an existing, large-scale database. The representative approach for this task is to develop a semantic parser (of questions), which will be the main focus. Other approaches like text matching in the embedding space and those driven by information extraction will also be discussed. The other category, *QA with the Web*, targets answering questions using mainly from the facts extracted from general text corpora derived from the Web. In addition to the common components and techniques used in this setting, including passage retrieval, entity recognition and question analysis, we will also introduce latest work on how to leverage and incorporate additional structured and semi-structured data to improve the performance. The third category of the QA problems that we will highlight is the non-factoid questions. Due to its broad coverage, we will briefly cover three exemplary topics: story comprehension, reasoning questions and paragraph QA. The tutorial will conclude by summarizing a whole area of exciting and dynamic research that is worthy of more detailed investigation for many years to come.

Outline

Part I. Overview of Question Answering Research

- Overview of early Question Answering research
    - Natural language understanding problems proposed at the dawn of AI

Proceedings of NAACL-HLT 2016, pages 8–10,
San Diego, California, June 12-17, 2016.

    - Early representative QA systems
    - Key developments and milestones
- Current Question Answering research trend
    - Categories of QA problems and settings studied recently
    - Data sources, technical problems and solutions
    - Main challenges and opportunities
- Demos of some existing QA systems

Part II. Question Answering with Knowledge Base

- Introduction to modern large-scale knowledge base
- Task setting and benchmark datasets
- State-of-the-art approaches
    - Semantic parsing (of questions)
    - Matching questions and answers in embedding space
    - Information extraction and text matching

Part III. Question Answering with the Web

- Problem setting and the general system architecture
- Essential natural language analysis: entity and answer type
- Leveraging additional information sources
    - Usage data (e.g., search query logs or browsing logs)
    - Knowledge bases
    - Semi-structured data (e.g., Web tables)

Part IV. Non-Factoid Question Answering

- Story comprehension (e.g., MC-Test)
- Reasoning questions (e.g., bAbI dataset & task)
- Paragraph QA (e.g., quiz bowl competition)

Part V. Conclusion

Instructor bios

Scott Wen-tau Yih is a Senior Researcher at Microsoft Research Redmond. His research interests include natural language processing, machine learning and information retrieval. Yih received his Ph.D. in computer science at the University of Illinois at Urbana-Champaign. His work on joint inference using integer linear programming (ILP) [Roth & Yih, 2004] helped the UIUC team win the CoNLL-05 shared task on semantic role labeling, and the approach has been widely adopted in the NLP community since then. After joining MSR in 2005, he has worked on email spam filtering, keyword extraction and search & ad relevance. His recent work focuses on continuous semantic representations using neural networks and matrix/tensor decomposition methods, with applications in lexical semantics, knowledge base embedding and question answering. Yih received the best paper award from CoNLL-2011, an outstanding paper award from ACL-2015 and has served as area chairs (HLT-NAACL-12, ACL-14, EMNLP-16), program co-chairs (CEAS-09, CoNLL-14) and action editor (Transactions of ACL) in recent years.

Hao Ma is a Researcher at Microsoft Research, Redmond, WA, USA. He obtained his Ph.D. in Computer Science at The Chinese University of Hong Kong. His research interests include Information Retrieval, Natural Language Processing, Machine Learning, Recommender Systems and Social Network Analysis. Most recently, Dr. Ma has been working on entity related research problems and applications. He designed the core learning algorithms that powered both Bing's and Microsoft's entity experience, including question answering, entity recommendation, attributes ranking, interpretation, exploration, carousel ranking, etc. He has published more than 40 research papers in prestigious conferences and journals, including WWW, SIGIR, WSDM, AAAI, TOIS, TKDE, TMM, TIST, etc. Some of his research work has been widely reported by popular news media, like MIT Technology Review, Search Engine Land, etc. Dr. Ma is also in the winning team that won the Microposts Entity Linking Challenge in WWW 2014.

Recent Progress in Deep Learning for NLP

Instructors: Zhengdong Lu and Hang Li

Abstract:

Neural network-based methods have been viewed as one of the major driving force in the recent development of natural language processing (NLP). We all have witnessed with great excitement how this subfield advances: new ideas emerge at an unprecedented speed and old ideas resurge in unexpected ways. In a nutshell, there are two major trends:

- Ideas and techniques from other fields of machine learning and artificial intelligence (A.I.) have increasing impact on neural network-based NLP methods.
- With end-to-end models taking on more complex tasks, the design of architecture and mechanisms often needs more domain knowledge from linguists and other domain experts.

Both trends are important to researchers in the computational linguistics community. Fundamental ideas like external memory or reinforcement learning, although introduced to NLP only recently, have quickly lead to significant improvement on tasks like natural language generation and question answering. On the other hand, with complicated neural systems with many cooperating components, it calls for linguistic knowledge in designing the right mechanism, architecture, and sometimes training setting.

As a simple example, the introducing of automatic alignment in neural machine translation, has quickly led to the state-of-the-art performance in machine translation and triggered a large body of sequence-to-sequence models. It is therefore important to get the researchers in computational linguistics community acquainted with the recent progress in deep learning for NLP.

We will focus on the work and ideas strongly related to the core of natural language and yet not so familiar to the majority of the community, which can be roughly categorized into: 1) the differentiable data-structures, and 2) the learning paradigms for NLP.

Differentiable data-structures, starting with the memory equipped with continuous operations in Neural Turing Machine, have been the foundation of deep models with sophisticated operations. Some members of it, such as Memory Network, have become famous on tasks like question answering and machine translation, while other development in this direction, including those with clear and important application in NLP, are relatively new to this community.

Deep learning, with its promise on end-to-end learning, not only enables the training of complex NLP models from scratch, but also extends the training setting to include remote and indirect supervision. We will introduce not only the end-to-end learning in its general notion, but also newly emerged topics in formulating learning objective, taming the non-differentiable operations, and designing the learning system for getting supervision signal from real world.

Outline:

- Part I: Overview (30 minutes)
  - Basic concepts and techniques in deep learning for NLP
  - A brief summary of recent progress
- Part II: Differentiable data-structures for NLP (one hour)
  - External memory, reading and writing, attention
  - Short-term memory, episodic memory, and long-term memory
  - Structures in memory, deep memory-based architectures
  - Application on machine translation and dialogue
  - Other differentiable data-structures
  - Neural stack and queue for sequence processing
  - Neural pointers for nonlinear data-structures, e.g., trees
- Part III: Learning paradigms (one hour)
  - End-to-end learning in general
  - Grounded language learning in neural models
  - Learning from execution: e.g., for semantic parsing in neural QA models
  - Grounding to other modalities, e.g., images
  - Reinforcement Learning in deep NLP models
  - For learning dialogue policy
  - For language generation
  - For other discrete choices in neural language models, e.g., memory-access
  - Other non-differentiable choices in learning deep NLP models, eg. Minimum risk training
- Part IV: Conclusion

About the Instructors:

Zhengdong Lu is a senior researcher at Noah's Ark Lab, Huawei Technologies. His research interests are neural network-based methods for natural language processing, including dialogue, machine translation, semantic parsing, and reasoning. Previously he was an associate researcher at Microsoft Research Asia and a postdoctoral researcher at University of Texas at Austin, after receiving his Ph.D.degree from Oregon Health and Science University in 2008 in computer science. He has published over 30 papers in prestigious journals and conferences, including NIPS, ICML, ACL, KDD, IJCAI and AAAI, including over 10 recent papers on deep learning methods for NLP and AI.

Hang Li is director of the Noah's Ark Lab of Huawei Technologies, adjunct professors of Peking University and Nanjing University. His research areas include information retrieval, natural language processing, statistical machine learning, and data mining. He is ACM Distinguished Scientist. Hang graduated from Kyoto University in 1988 and earned his PhD from the University of Tokyo in 1998. He worked at the NEC lab as researcher during 1991 and 2001, and Microsoft Research Asia as senior researcher and research manager during 2001 and 2012. He joined Huawei Technologies in 2012. Hang has published three technical books, and more than 100 technical papers at top international conferences including SIGIR, WWW, WSDM, ACL, EMNLP, ICML, NIPS, SIGKDD and top international journals including CL, NLE, JMLR, TOIS, IRJ, IPM, TKDE, TWEB, TIST. He and his colleague's papers received the SIGKDD-08 best application paper award, the SIGIR-08 best student paper award, the ACL-12 best student paper award. Hang worked on the development of several products such as Microsoft SQL Server 2005, Office 2007, Office 2010, Live Search 2008, Bing 2009, Bing 2010, Huawei AppStore, Huawei Phones. He has 40 granted US patents. Hang is also very active in the research communities and has served or is serving top international conferences as PC chair, Senior PC member, or PC member, including SIGIR, WWW, WSDM, ACL, EMNLP, NIPS, SIGKDD, ICDM, ACML, and top international journals as associate editor or editorial board member, including CL, IRJ, TIST, JASIST, JCST. Hang Li gave a number of tutorials on various topics about machine learning for natural language processing and information retrieval, including a tutorial on learning to rank at ACL 2009.

Scalable Statistical Relational Learning for NLP

Instructors: William Yang Wang and William W. Cohen

Prerequisites: No prior knowledge of statistical relational learning is required.

Abstract:

Statistical Relational Learning (SRL) is an interdisciplinary research area that combines first-order logic and machine learning methods for probabilistic inference. Although many Natural Language Processing (NLP) tasks (including text classification, semantic parsing, information extraction, coreference resolution, and sentiment analysis) can be formulated as inference in a first-order logic, most probabilistic first-order logics are not efficient enough to be used for large-scale versions of these tasks. In this tutorial, we provide a gentle introduction to the theoretical foundation of probabilistic logics, as well as their applications in NLP. We describe recent advances in designing scalable probabilistic logics, with a special focus on ProPPR. Finally, we provide a hands-on demo about scalable probabilistic logic programming for solving practical NLP problems.

Outline:

- **Part 1: Foundations and Applications of Probabilistic First-Order Logic**
- We will provide a brief review of some first-order learning systems that have been developed in the past: Markov Logic Networks (Richardson and Domingos, 2006), Stochastic Logic Programs (Muggleton, 1996). In this part, we introduce the semantics of the above languages with their inference (and learning) approaches. We analyze and discuss the core ideas behind of such language. We show various applications of probabilistic logics in NLP.
- **Part 2: Scalable Probabilistic Logics: A Case Study of ProPPR.**
- We will focus on the efficiency issue, and introduce recent advances of scalable probabilistic logics, including lifted inference techniques (Van den Broeck and Suciu, 2014) and probabilistic soft logic (Bach et al., 2015). In particular, we will take CMU's ProPPR (Wang et al., 2013) as a case study. We describe the main contributions of ProPPR: including its approximate personalized PageRank inference scheme, parallel stochastic gradient descent learning method, and its flexibility in theory engineering. We then introduce the structure learning methods in ProPPR (Wang et al., CIKM 2014), including a structured regularization method as an alternative to predicate invention (Wang et al., IJCAI 2015). We will also cover our latest attempt of learning first-order logic formula embeddings, and discuss its relationship to (and possible connections between) even newer approaches to modeling knowledge bases, relationships, and inference using deep learning methods. To conclude this part, we show an interesting application of ProPPR (Wang et al., ACL-IJCNLP 2015): a joint information extraction and knowledge reasoning engine.
- **Part 3: Demos and Practical Applications.**

- We switch from the theoretical presentations to an interactive demonstration session: we aim at providing a hands-on lab session to transfer the theories of scalable probabilistic logics into practices. More specifically, we will provide a demo of several applications on synthetic and real-world datasets. Participants are encouraged to check out our repository on Github (https://github.com/TeamCohen/ProPPR) and bring laptops to the tutorial. The list of demo examples to be considered are text categorization, entity resolution, knowledge base completion (Wang et al., MLJ 2015), dependency parsing (Wang et al., EMNLP 2014), structure learning, and joint information extraction & reasoning.

About the Instructors:

William Yang Wang: Carnegie Mellon University, yww@cs.cmu.edu, http://www.cs.cmu.edu/~yww/

William Wang is a final-year PhD student at the School of Computer Science, Carnegie Mellon University. He works with William Cohen on designing scalable learning and inference algorithms for statistical relational learning, knowledge reasoning, and information extraction. He has published about 30 papers at leading conferences and journals including ACL, EMNLP, and NAACL. He has received best paper awards (or nominations) at ASRU, CIKM, and EMNLP, a best reviewer award at NAACL 2015, the Richard King Mellon Presidential Fellowship in 2011, and he is a Facebook Fellowship finalist. He is an alumnus of Columbia University, and a former research scientist intern at Yahoo! Labs, Microsoft Research Redmond, and University of Southern California.

William W. Cohen: Carnegie Mellon University, wcohen@cs.cmu.edu, http://www.cs.cmu.edu/~wcohen/

William Cohen is a professor of machine learning at Carnegie Mellon University. Dr. Cohen's research interests include information integration and machine learning, particularly information extraction, text categorization and learning from large datasets. He has a long-standing interest in statistical relational learning and learning models, or learning from data, that display non-trivial structure. He holds seven patents related to learning, discovery, information retrieval, and data integration, and is the author of more than 200 publications. He was a past president of International Machine Learning Society. He is a AAAI fellow, and was a winner of SIGMOD Test of Time Award and SIGIR Test of Time Award.

References:

Richardson, Matthew, and Pedro Domingos. "Markov logic networks."Machine learning 62.1-2 (2006): 107-136.

Muggleton, Stephen. "Stochastic logic programs." Advances in inductive logic programming 32 (1996): 254-264.

Van den Broeck, G., and Dan Suciu. "Lifted probabilistic inference in relational models." UAI tutorials (2014).

Bach, Stephen H., et al. "Hinge-loss Markov random fields and probabilistic soft logic." arXiv preprint arXiv:1505.04406 (2015).

Wang, William Yang, Kathryn Mazaitis, and William W. Cohen. "Programming with personalized pagerank: a locally groundable first-order probabilistic logic." Proceedings of the 22nd ACM international conference on Conference on information & knowledge management. ACM, 2013.

Wang, William Yang, Kathryn Mazaitis, and William W. Cohen. "Structure learning via parameter learning." Proceedings of the 23rd ACM International Conference on Conference on Information and Knowledge Management. ACM, 2014.

Wang, William Yang, Kathryn Mazaitis, and William W. Cohen. "A soft version of predicate invention based on structured sparsity." Proceedings of the 24th International Joint Conference on Artificial Intelligence (IJCAI 2015), Buenos Aires, Argentina. 2015.

Wang, William Yang, and William W. Cohen. "Joint information extraction and reasoning: A scalable statistical relational learning approach."Proceedings of the 53rd Annual Meeting of the Association for Computational Linguistics and The 7th International Joint Conference of the Asian Federation of Natural Language Processing (ACL-IJCNLP 2015), Beijing, China. 2015.

Wang, William Yang, et al. "Efficient inference and learning in a large knowledge base." Machine Learning 100.1 (2015): 101-126.

William Yang Wang, Lingpeng Kong, Kathryn Mazaitis, and William W. Cohen, "Dependency Parsing for Weibo: An Efficient Probabilistic Logic Programming Approach", in Proceedings of the Conference on Empirical Methods in Natural Language Processing (EMNLP 2014), short paper, Doha, Qatar, Oct. 25-29, 2014, ACL.

Statistical Machine Translation between Related Languages

Instructors: Pushpak Bhattacharyya, Mitesh Khapra, and Anoop Kunchukuttan

Prerequisites: Basic knowledge of statistical machine translation

Abstract:

Language-independent Statistical Machine Translation (SMT) has proven to be very challenging. The diversity of languages makes high accuracy difficult and requires substantial parallel corpus as well as linguistic resources (parsers, morph analyzers, etc.). An interesting observation is that a large chunk of machine translation (MT) requirements involve related languages. They are either : (i) between related languages, or (ii) between a lingua franca (like English) and a set of related languages. For instance, India, the European Union and South-East Asia have such translation requirements due to government, business and socio-cultural communication needs.

Related languages share a lot of linguistic features and the divergences among them are at a lower level of the NLP pipeline. The objective of the tutorial is to discuss how the relatedness among languages can be leveraged to bridge this language divergence thereby achieving some/all of these goals: (i) improving translation quality, (ii) achieving better generalization, (iii) sharing linguistic resources, and (iv) reducing resource requirements.

We will look at the existing research in SMT from the perspective of related languages, with the goal to build a toolbox of methods that are useful for translation between related languages. This tutorial would be relevant to Machine Translation researchers and developers, especially those interested in translation between low-resource languages which have resource-rich related languages. It will also be relevant for researchers interested in multilingual computation.

We start with a motivation for looking at the SMT problem from the perspective of related languages. We introduce notions of language relatedness useful for MT. We explore how lexical, morphological and syntactic similarity among related languages can help MT. Lexical similarity will receive special attention since related languages share a significant vocabulary in terms of cognates, loanwords, etc.

Then, we look beyond bilingual MT and present how pivot-based and multi-source methods incorporate knowledge from multiple languages, and handle language pairs lacking parallel corpora. We present some studies concerning the implications of languages relatedness to pivot-based SMT, and ways of handling language divergence in the pivot-based SMT scenario. Recent advances in deep learning have made it possible to train multi-language neural MT systems, which we think would be relevant to training between related languages.

We will summarize the tutorial by pointing out how the toolbox addresses the following goals we set out: (i) improving translation quality, (ii) achieving better generalization, (iii) sharing linguistic resources, and (iv) reducing resource requirements. We will conclude by emphasizing how the toolbox can be used to design translation system architectures customized to a set of related languages.

Time permitting, we will briefly describe a toolkit for Indian language NLP, which can be used to leverage similarities between Indian languages (http://anoopkunchukuttan.github.io/indic_nlp_library).

Outline:

- Introduction
- Motivation
- Important questions
- Useful notions of language relatedness
- Leveraging lexical similarity for translation:
- Phonetic and Orthographic Similarity
- Transliteration & Cognate Mining
- Integrating transliteration & translation in decoder
- Transliteration of OOV words
- Translation using Transliteration (character-level translation)
- Neural character-level translation
- Leveraging morphological and syntactic similarity for translation:
- Morphological Isomorphism
- Common source reordering solution for a set of related languages
- Synergy among languages:
- Pivot-based Methods
- Combining pivot-based and character-level SMT
- Multi-source translation
- Multi-lingual word alignment
- Multilingual translation with Neural MT

About the Instructors:

Dr. Pushpak Bhattacharyya

Professor, Dept. of Computer Science & Engineering, Indian Institute of Technology Bombay

Mumbai, India.

e-mail: pb@cse.iitb.ac.in

Website: https://www.cse.iitb.ac.in/~pb

Dr. Pushpak Bhattacharyya is Vijay and Sita Vashee Chair Professor in the Department of Computer Science and Engineering at the Indian Institute of Technology Bombay (IITB) where he heads the Center for Natural Language Processing. He is also the Director of Indian Institute of Technology Patna.

Dr. Bhattacharyya obtained his Ph.D from IIT Bombay. His areas of interest cover a broad spectrum of problems in Natural Language Processing like machine translation, cross-lingual search, sentiment analysis - specially with reference to Indian languages.

Dr. Bhattacharyya has published extensively in top quality conferences and journals (about 200). He has also written a textbook on machine translation. He has advised 12 PhDs in NLP and ML, and is currently supervising 10 PhD students. He has also advised close to 125 masters students and above 40 bachelor degree students for their research work.

Dr. Mitesh Khapra

Researcher, IBM India Research Laboratory,

Bangalore, India.

e-mail: mikhapra@in.ibm.com

Website: http://researcher.watson.ibm.com/researcher/view.php?person=in-mikhapra

Mitesh Khapra obtained his Ph.D. from the Indian Institute of Technology Bombay in the area of Natural Language Processing with a focus on reusing resources for multilingual computation. His areas of interest include Statistical Machine Translation, Text Analytics, Crowdsourcing, Argument Mining and Deep Learning. He is currently working as a researcher at IBM Research India where he is focusing on mining arguments from large unstructured text. He has co-authored papers in NLP and ML conferences such as ACL, NAACL, EMNLP, AAAI and NIPS.

Anoop Kunchukuttan

Ph.D Scholar, Center for Indian Language Technology,

Dept. of Computer Science & Engineering, Indian Institute of Technology Bombay

Mumbai, India.

e-mail: anoopk@cse.iitb.ac.in

Website: www.cse.iitb.ac.in/~anoopk

Anoop Kunchukuttan is a senior Ph.D student at the Indian Institute of Technology Bombay. He is advised by Prof. Pushpak Bhattacharyya on his research work involving machine translation and transliteration among related languages. He has also investigated other NLP problems - multiword extraction, grammar correction, crowdsourcing and information extraction. He has co-authored papers in NLP conferences such as ACL, NAACL, CONLL, LREC, ICON. He has worked in the software industry for about 5 years, during which he led the development of large scale systems for information extraction and retrieval over medical text. He completed his M.Tech in Computer Science & Engineering from IIT Bombay.

Association for Computational Linguistics
209 N. Eighth Street
Stroudsburg, Pennsylvania 18360

ISBN 978-1-5108-2515-4

CURRAN ASSOCIATES INC.
proceedings.com